ONCE

UPON A TIME

"A BOOK FOR ALL AGES"

TABLE OF CONTENTS

ONCE UPON A TIME

ONCE UPON A TIME
THIS POET WROTE THIS BOOK
AN ENDEAVOR OF INSPIRATION
THAT HE UNDERTOOK

IN HOPE THAT ONE DAY
IT WILL BE
A BOOK THAT EVERYONE
WOULD LIKE TO READ

MAY EACH POEM
PUT A SMILE ON YOUR FACE
A SMILE THAT COMES FROM
BEING ABLE TO RELATE

AND IN EACH POEM
I HOPE YOU WILL SEE
ONCE UPON A TIME
IS REALITY

THE WISE TREE

ONCE UPON A TIME
THERE LIVED A WISE TREE
IT COULD BE ANYTHING
THAT IT WANTED TO BE

YET NOT ONCE
DID THE TREE CHANGE
THE TREE CHOSE
TO REMAIN THE SAME

THE TREE WAS ALSO
VERY WISE
FOR IN ORDER TO CHANGE
IT WOULD HAVE TO DIE

IT'S BETTER TO BRANCH OUT
INTO SOMETHING NEW
THAN TO CHANGE
AND KILL THE REAL YOU

A MYSTIC VOYAGE

ONCE UPON A TIME
UPON A MYSTICAL SEA
A SHIP SAILED
INTO ETERNITY

UPON A VOYAGE
THROUGH THE PASSAGE OF TIME
SAILING TO MANY WORLDS
OF MANY DIFFERENT KINDS

BEHOLDING THE SPECTRUM
OF IMMORTAL LIFE
SAILING BY DAY
SAILING BY NIGHT

A ENDLESS VOYAGE
UPON A ENDLESS SEA
SAILING UPON
A ENDLESS DESTINY

THOSE WHO
MISSED THE BOAT
REMAINED IN A WORLD
WITHOUT HOPE

A PLACE WITHOUT A TRACE

ONCE UPON A TIME
THERE WAS A PLACE
OF WHICH TODAY
THERE IS NO TRACE

RUMOR HAS IT
THE PLACE IS STILL THERE
AND HAS BEEN SEEN
THROUGHOUT THE YEARS

RUMORS OF SUCH PLACES
HAVE BEEN HEARD BEFORE
OF WHICH ONE
CAN NEVER BE SURE

BUT FOR THOSE OF US
WHO DO BELIEVE
SUCH PLACES
WILL ALWAYS BE

GODS' KINGDOM
IS SUCH A PLACE
THAT CAN ONLY BE SEEN
BY THOSE WHO HAVE FAITH

THERE WILL ALWAYS BE
THOSE IN DOUBT
IN SUCH PLACES
THEY WILL BE LEFT OUT

A MATTER OF PRIDE

ONCE UPON A TIME
IN AN EFFORT TO THRIVE
IT CAME DOWN
TO A MATTER OF PRIDE

TYPICAL OF
A TYPICAL MAN
THINKING THAT
HE'S IN COMMAND

ALLOWING PRIDE
TO HAVE ITS' WAY
IN ALL HE DOES
AND ALL HE SAYS

IN AN ALL OUT EFFORT
TO THRIVE
HE LOST IT ALL
IN A SEA OF PRIDE

AUTUMN

ONCE UPON A TIME
ONE AUTUMN DAY
AUTUMN GOT WIND
THAT WINTER WAS ON THE WAY

AUTUMN WAS TIRED
OF LOSING ITS' GROUND
EVERY TIME WINTER
WANTS TO COME AROUND

AUTUMN ORDINARILY
WAS PRETTY COOL
BUT WINTER WAS MAKING AUTUMN
LOOK LIKE A FOOL

AUTUMN WANTED
TO BE RELIABLE
SO AUTUMN WENT TO
WINTERS' ARCHRIVAL

SUMMER AGREED
TO LEND AUTUMN A HAND
AND INDIAN SUMMERS
BECAME KNOWN IN THE LAND

OLD MAN WINTER

ONCE UPON A TIME
ONE WINTER DAY
OLD MAN WINTER
HAD THIS TO SAY

I DON'T MEAN
TO BE SO COLD
IT'S JUST MY NATURE
FROM TIMES OF OLD

NO MATTER HOW NICE
I TRY TO BE
MY NATURE
GETS THE BEST OF ME

ON MANY OCCASIONS
I TRIED TO CHANGE
IN THE PLACE OF SNOW
I PUT RAIN

BUT IT ONLY
MAKES MATTERS WORST
WHEN IT FREEZES
PEOPLE GET HURT

MY HAZARDOUS CONDITIONS
FAIL TO IMPROVE
NO MATTER WHAT
I TRY TO DO

AGE & TIME

ONCE UPON A TIME
AGE SPOKE WITH TIME
AGE SAID I AM YOURS
AND YOU ARE MINES

BUT I CAN'T DO
WHAT YOU CAN
YET YOU ARE
WHAT I AM

WHY DO YOU SURPASS ME
BY FAR
WHEN I'M A MANIFESTATION
OF WHAT YOU ARE

TIME REPLIED
YOU ARE AS GREAT AS I
FOR WITHOUT YOU
I WOULD DIE

YOU ARE THE CYCLE
OF MY LIFE
YOU ARE THE DAY
YOU ARE THE NIGHT

SEEDS OF GOOD DEEDS

ONCE UPON A TIME
A MAN SOWED HIS SEEDS
IN A FIELD
OF GOOD DEEDS

THE SOIL THERE
WAS VERY RICH
AND SO WAS
HIS HARVEST

THE FRIENDSHIP

ONCE UPON A TIME
UPON THE HIGH SEAS
"THE FRIENDSHIP" SAILED
INTO HISTORY

CAUGHT IN THE MIDST
OF A STORM
"THE FRIENDSHIP" WAS
BADLY TORN

THE STORM PASSED OVER
AND THE SUN CAME OUT
LEAVING "THE FRIENDSHIP"
IN SERIOUS DOUBT

THE DAMAGE WAS NOT
BEYOND REPAIR
PROVIDED IT COULD GET
IMMEDIATE CARE

BUT CARE WAS NOWHERE
TO BE FOUND
SO "THE FRIENDSHIP"
WENT DOWN

IT COULD BE SALVAGED
AT A LATER TIME
BUT "THE FRIENDSHIP" MIGHT BE
TOO HARD TO FIND

THE DISCOVERY OF LOVE

ONCE UPON A TIME
TWO PEOPLE DISCOVERED LOVE
AND SPENT THEIR LIVES
LEARNING WHAT IT WAS

THEY DISCOVERED LOVE
AT FIRST SIGHT
THE CHEMISTRY BETWEEN THEM
WAS JUST RIGHT

NOW THE TEST
WAS TO SEE
THE DEGREE
OF COMPATIBILITY

THEY COMPARED NOTES
WITH ONE ANOTHER
AND HE AND SHE
BECAME LOVERS

ENTERING INTO PHASE TWO
THE TEST OF TIME
WOULD THERE BE
A CHANGE OF MIND

THEIR LOVE TOOK ON
A CONSISTENT NATURE
WHICH THEY DOCUMENTED
ON A CERTIFICATE OF PAPER

HAPPILY MARRIED
THEY ENTERED INTO PHASE THREE
THE TEST
OF BEING A FAMILY

THIS WAS TO BE
THE FINAL TEST
UPON WHICH ALL THEIR LOVE
WOULD COME TO REST

IT MEANT TAKING ALL
THEY LEARNED BEFORE
AND MAKING THE ANALYSES
JUST ONE TIME MORE

HIGHER SELF

ONCE UPON A TIME
IN A MYSTICAL LAND
EXISTED THE WAY
OF THE HIGHER MAN

FREEDOM FROM
THE BONDAGE OF FLESH
STRIVING TO
ATTAIN ONES' BEST

LEARNING BY
THE EXPERIENCE OF LIFE
ATTAINING WISDOM
ATTAINING INSIGHT

PEACE AND HARMONY
WITHIN ALL THINGS
ENJOYING THE HAPPINESS
THAT IT BRINGS

PRACTICING DAILY
WAYS TO ATTAIN
THE SECRETS
OF THE HIGHER PLANE

A INNOCENT MAN

ONCE UPON A TIME
A DECISION WAS MADE
TO SEND A INNOCENT MAN
TO HIS GRAVE

A GREAT INJUSTICE
HAD BEEN DONE
THAT WOULD AFFECT
THE LIVES OF EVERYONE

HE MAINTAINED HIS INNOCENCE
UNTIL THE END
AND VOWED THAT HE
WOULD LIVE AGAIN

BUT NOBODY LISTENED
NOBODY TOOK HEED
TO HIS VOW
OR TO HIS PLEA

ON THE DAY
HE WAS PUT TO DEATH
THE MANS' SOUL
DID NOT REST

NEITHER DID THE PEOPLE
OF THE TOWN
FOR THAT INNOCENT MAN
WILL ALWAYS BE AROUND

THE MORAL
OF THE STORY IS
NEVER CONDEMN A INNOCENT MAN
WHO WANTS TO LIVE

THE STAR TO SEE

ONCE UPON A TIME
A STAR APPEARED
A STAR UNLIKE ANY
IN THE ATMOSPHERE

IT HAS NEVER APPEARED
IN THE SAME PLACE TWICE
MAKING IF DIFFICULT
TO CATCH A GLIMPSE OF ITS' LIGHT

TO SEE THE LIGHT
OF THIS STAR SHINE
YOU HAVE TO BE IN THE RIGHT PLACE
AT THE RIGHT TIME

FOR IT IS
THE STAR OF SUCCESS
DIFFERENT FROM
ALL THE REST

THE MAGICAL STREAM

ONCE UPON A TIME
THERE WAS A MAGICAL STREAM
SAID TO HAVE POWERS
TO DO WONDERFUL THINGS

PEOPLE CAME FROM
MILES AROUND
SEEKING WHERE THE STREAM
COULD BE FOUND

THE JOURNEY TO THE STREAM
WAS A JOURNEY OF FAITH
A JOURNEY THAT EVERYONE
COULD NOT MAKE

FOR THOSE PEOPLE
WHO CAME TO PRAY
THE MAGICAL STREAM
WAS NEVER FAR AWAY

JOURNEY IN A DISTANT MIND

ONCE UPON A DISTANT PLANET
IN A DISTANT TIME
PEOPLE HAVE JOURNEYED
IN THE REGIONS OF THEIR MIND

THERE THEY CAME FACE TO FACE
WITH THEMSELVES
IN A PLACE
WHERE THEY NEEDED HELP

THE ENCOUNTER
WAS OF THE THIRD KIND
AN ALIEN BEING
WITHIN THEIR OWN MIND

WHOS' WORLD SEEMED
SO FAR AWAY
YET THEY TRAVELED THERE
EVERY DAY

THE TERRAIN WAS VIRTUALLY
UNKNOWN TO THEM
YET THEY VAGUELY FELT
THEY HAD BEEN OVER THEM

IT WAS A NEW WORLD
AS FAR AS THEY COULD SEE
UNTIL ONE DAY
THEY STUMBLED UPON REALITY

THAT DAY THEIR JOURNEY
CAME TO AN END
BUT THEY WERE SO SPACED OUT
THEY KNEW NOT WHERE TO BEGIN

THEIR JOURNEY BACK
WAS GOING TO BE ROUGH
FOR THEY HAD FALLEN
INTO A DEEP RUT

THEY WERE ALL ALONE
WITH NO ONE TO CARE
THEY HAD NO ONE TO HELP THEM
GET OUT OF THERE

THEN ALONG CAME AN ALIEN
AND GAVE THEM A HAND
HE BROUGHT THEM BACK
FROM NO MANS' LAND

IN AN ALIEN LAND
NOT OF THEIR OWN

THE ALIEN WAS THEMSELVES
A PART UNKNOWN

THE COOL SCHOOL

ONCE UPON A TIME
I HEARD OF A SCHOOL
THAT TAUGHT THE KIDS
TO BE HIP AND COOL

CLASSES WERE HELD
IN THE STREETS
CLASS IN SESSION
SEVEN DAYS A WEEK

THE STUDENT BODY
WAS A GANG
ENGLISH WAS TAUGHT
IN THE FORM OF SLANG

HISTORY WAS CRIMINALS
PAST RECORDS OF CRIME
MATH WAS TAUGHT
IN DOLLAR SIGNS

PENMANSHIP WAS JUDGED
BY THE FORGING OF A NAME
AND BREAKING THE RULES
THE NAME OF THE GAME

THE HOUSE OF LIFE

ONCE UPON A TIME
THERE WAS A HOUSE
CONTAINING ALL
THAT LIFE WAS ABOUT

ALTHOUGH THE HOUSE
WAS LIVED IN BY MANY
IT WAS NEVER
OWNED BY ANY

BECAUSE NO ONE
COULD AFFORD
ANYTHING MORE THAN
ROOM AND BOARD

IT'S KNOWN AS PAYING
OUR WAY THROUGH LIFE
WITHIN OUR SOUL
WE PAY THE PRICE

A PLACE CALLED FAME

ONCE UPON A TIME
THERE WAS A PLACE CALLED FAME
A FAMOUS PLACE
BY WAY OF ITS' NAME

FOUNDED BY PEOPLE
OF A SPECIAL BREED
BY ACHIEVEMENT
OF OUTSTANDING DEEDS

BY THE INDIVIDUAL EFFORT
OF EACH ONE
THE BUILDING OF FAME
WAS BEGUN

BY SKILL
AND DETERMINATION
FAME BECAME KNOWN
THROUGHOUT THE NATIONS

A GREAT LIGHT

ONCE UPON A TIME
THERE WAS A GREAT LIGHT
YET IT DIDN'T SHINE
VERY BRIGHT

FOR ITS' GREATNESS WAS NOT
A MEASURE OF ITSELF
ITS' POWER WAS IN
SOMETHING ELSE

ALTHOUGH ITS' RADIANCE
WAS EXCEEDED BY MANY
IT CONTINUED TO SHINE
WHEN THERE WEREN'T ANY

ITS' GREATNESS CAN BE APPLIED
TO MANY THINGS
ESPECIALLY IN THE LIGHT OF US
AS HUMAN BEINGS

THE MAGICIAN

ONCE UPON A TIME
THERE WAS A REAL MAGICIAN
THAT EXISTED
IN ANOTHER DIMENSION

BY THE POWER
OF THE UNIVERSAL MIND
THE MAGICIAN TRAVELED
THROUGH SPACE AND TIME

EARTH WAS A PLACE
ALONG THE WAY
WHERE THE MAGICIAN
ONCE STAYED

THE ROAD TO ANYWHERE

ONCE UPON A TIME
THERE WAS A ROAD
THAT COULD TAKE YOU ANYWHERE
YOU WANTED TO GO

IT APPEARED IN MANY DIFFERENT PLACES
AT MANY DIFFERENT TIMES
BUT IT ALWAYS ORIGINATED
WITHIN THE MIND

REALITY

ONCE UPON A TIME
THERE CAME TO BE
THIS THING
WE CALL "REALITY"

THAT WHICH SEEMED
TO BE REAL
SAT UPON
A HIGH HILL

WHERE IT WAS
OUT OF REACH
FEW WERE IN TOUCH
NONE COULD KEEP

REALITY REMAINS
A BIT TOO HIGH
FOR MOST PEOPLE
TO LIVE BY

SETTING THERE
UPON THAT HILL
MANY LOOK AND SEE
BUT CAN NOT FEEL

ILLUSION & CONFUSION

ONCE UPON A TIME
IN A STATE OF ILLUSION
THE BIRTH TOOK PLACE
OF CONFUSION

THUS CONFUSION
CAME INTO BEING
AS ILLUSIONS'
OFFSPRING

BY ILLUSIONS' DISTORTION
OF WHAT IS TRUE
CONFUSION ALWAYS
COMES INTO VIEW

A NEW YEAR RESOLUTION

ONCE UPON A TIME
ONE NEW YEAR DAY
THIS NEW YEAR RESOLUTION
WAS MADE

THAT EACH 365 DAYS
OF THE YEAR
BE FULFILLED
WITH THE FIRST DAYS' GOOD CHEER

FOR EACH DAY IS A NEW DAY
AND BRINGS FORTH NEW LIFE
AND SHOULD BE CELEBRATED
WITH GREAT DELIGHT

A RESOLUTION TO BE HAPPY
IS WHAT IT IS
BY CELEBRATING EACH DAY
THAT WE LIVE

ESTRANGE

ONCE UPON A TIME
UPON THE PATH OF LIFE
TWO PEOPLE MET
AND BECAME HUSBAND AND WIFE

THEY LIVED IN A HOUSE
ALONG THE WAY
WHERE SOMETHING STRANGE
HAPPENED ONE DAY

THERE WAS A KNOCK
AT THE DOOR
SOMEONE THEY HAD NEVER
SEEN BEFORE

THE STRANGER ASKED
TO COME INSIDE
THE STRANGER ENTERED
AND THEIR LOVE DIED

INSTEAD OF PUTTING
THE STRANGER OUT
THEY ALLOWED THE STRANGER
TO ROAM ABOUT

BY THE TIME
THE STRANGER LEFT
THE COUPLES' LIFE
WAS IN A MESS

THE STRANGER HAD
BECOME THEIR FRIEND
BRINGING THEIR MARRIAGE
TO AN END

THE HOUSE THEY LIVED IN
IS STILL THERE
THE RESIDENCE OF MANY COUPLES
DOWN THROUGH THE YEARS

A WORLD FORSEEN

ONCE UPON A TIME
IT WAS FORSEEN
A WORLD ABUNDANT
IN EVERYTHING

AND THAT MANKIND
WOULD FIND ITS' WAY
IN A WORLD WHERE MANY
WOULD BE LED ASTRAY

UNLIMITED WOULD MANKIND
ONE DAY BE
BY THEIR KNOWLEDGE
SHALL THEY BE SET FREE

GLORIOUS
BEYOND ALL BELIEF
YET FILLED WITH SUFFERING
AND FILLED WITH GRIEF

FOR ITS' A WORLD OF GOOD
AND A WORLD OF EVIL
A WORLD OF PEACE
AND A WORLD OF UPHEAVAL

GREAT
SHALL THEY BOTH BE
IN THIS WORLD
OF OPPOSITE REALITY

A DARK & SILENT NIGHT

ONCE UPON A TIME
ONE DARK AND SILENT NIGHT
THERE CAME FORTH
A BRILLIANT LIGHT

IN THE MANIFESTATION
OF CONCEIVED THOUGHT
A RAY OF LIGHT
IT WAS NOT

IT WAS LIGHT
OF A DIFFERENT KIND
SHINNING WITHIN THE ANNALS
OF THE MIND

UPON A DARK
AND SILENT NIGHT
I RECEIVED
THIS INSIGHT

THE SACRED KEY

ONCE UPON A TIME
THERE WAS A SACRED KEY
THAT COULD UNLOCK
THE DOOR OF MYSTERY

ONE DAY THE DOOR LOCKED
WITH THE KEY INSIDE
LOCKING AWAY FOREVER
THE MYSTERIES OF OUR LIVES

THERE WAS ONLY
ONE SACRED KEY
NOW IT'S AMONG
THE MYSTERIES

A WISE PRINCE

ONCE UPON A TIME
A KINGDOM WAS SAVED
BY A WISE PRINCE
OF THEIR DAY

THE KINGDOM WAS UNDER
CONSTANT ATTACK
BUT THE PEOPLE REFUSED
TO FIGHT BACK

NOW THE PRINCE
WHO WAS TO BECOME KING
KNEW HE HAD TO
CHANGE THINGS

SO HE GAVE HIS PEOPLE
ALL OF HIMSELF
IN RETURN THEY FOUGHT
DESIRING TO HELP

YOU SEE THE KINGS
THAT RULED BEFORE
NEVER GAVE THE PEOPLE
A REASON TO FIGHT FOR

A SIGN

ONCE UPON A TIME
A PERSON FOR A SIGN
RIGHT THERE
BUT HARD TO FIND

THE SIGN
WAS IN DISGUISE
RIGHT BEFORE
THEIR EYES

BUT THEY
DID NOT SEE
THAT THE SIGN
WAS ME

A PERSON
THEY KNEW
BUT NEVER
REALLY LISTENED TO

A LOST PERSON

ONCE UPON A TIME
THIS PERSON LOST THEIR WAY
THE PATH THEY WERE ON
LED THEM ASTRAY

REALIZING THEY WERE LOST
THEY LOOKED ABOUT
AND FOUND THEMSELVES'
IN A WORLD OF DOUBT

FOR THEY HAD LOST
ALL DIRECTION
OF WHICH THEIR LIFE
WAS A REFLECTION

NO MATTER WHAT
DIRECTION THEY WENT
IT DID NOT MAKE
ANY SENSE

BEYOND THE LIMIT
OF SAVING THEMSELVES'
ANOTHER PARTY
WAS THEIR ONLY HELP

SOMEONE WHO COULD
BRING THEM BACK
AND PUT THEM ON
THE RIGHT TRACK

BLONDES USE TO HAVE MORE FUN

ONCE UPON A TIME
BLONDES HAD MORE FUN
THEY WERE THE MOST BEAUTIFUL WOMEN
UNDER THE SUN

THEN WOMEN BEGAN TO BE SEEN
IN A DIFFERENT LIGHT
IN WHICH THE BLONDE
DIDN'T SHINE AS BRIGHT

NOW WHEN A MAN
STOPS AND STARES
YOU CAN BET IT'S NOT
THE COLOR OF HER HAIR

AND WHEN IT COMES DOWN
TO HAVING SOME FUN
IT'S A PARTY
FOR EVERYONE

THE MEN OF TODAY
ARE COLOR BLIND
ALL WOMEN
LOOK JUST AS FINE

THE ROAD OF LIFE

ONCE UPON A TIME
THERE WAS A ROAD
PEOPLE TRAVELED
TO AND FRO

TRAVELED BY DAY
TRAVELED BY NIGHT
BY ALL PEOPLE
FROM ALL WALKS OF LIFE

THE ROAD LED
TO ALL DESTINATIONS
TRAVELED UPON
FOR ALL OCCASIONS

THEN ONE DAY
IT CEASED TO BE
AND TOOK ITS' PLACE
IN HISTORY

A SUPERSTAR

ONCE UPON A TIME
THERE WAS A SUPERSTAR
NEVER BEFORE HAD ONES' LIGHT
SHINED SO FAR

THE SUPERSTARS LIGHT
TRULY SHINED FROM HEAVEN
THEIR MUSIC
A DIVINE COLLECTION

IT WAS TRULY
AN ACT OF FATE
HOW THEIR MUSIC
MADE THEM SO GREAT

A LEGEND
IN THEIR OWN TIME
THIS STARS' LIGHT
WILL ALWAYS SHINE

IF YOU'RE EVER OUT
ON A CLEAR NIGHT
LOOK UP
AND YOU'LL SEE THE LIGHT

IT'S THE BRIGHTEST STAR
IN THE SKY
THE ONE THE OTHER STARS
ARE JAMMING BY

SET FREE

ONCE UPON A TIME
THIS PERSON WAS SET FREE
IN A WORLD
WITH NO SUCH DESTINY

THIS PERSON WAS AN EXCEPTION
TO THE RULE
IN A WORLD
DESIGNED FOR FOOLS

BY A MIRACLE
IN THIS PERSONS' LIFE
THIS PERSON FOUND FREEDOM
IN THE LIGHT

IN THE LIGHT
THIS PERSON WAS ABLE TO SEE
FROM A WORLD OF DARKNESS
THIS PERSON WAS SET FREE

THAT'S LIFE

ONCE UPON A TIME
A YOUTH VENTURED OUT
WANTING TO LEARN
WHAT LIFE IS ABOUT

AT THE AGE
OF MATURITY IN LIFE
WHAT THE YOUTH LEARNED
CAME WITH A PRICE

AS AN ADULT
IT WAS PLAIN TO SEE
WHAT THE YOUTH COULD HAVE
GROWN UP TO BE

A PLACE UNKNOWN

ONCE UPON A TIME
THERE WAS A PLACE
THAT WAS OFF LIMIT
TO THE HUMAN RACE

A PLACE WHERE NO HUMAN
HAD GONE BEFORE
IT WAS A PLACE
WITHOUT WAR

A MAN OF COURAGE

ONCE UPON A TIME
IN THE FACE OF DEATH
A MANS' COURAGE
WAS PUT TO THE TEST

FEAR SOUGHT
TO INVADE THE MAN
TO RENDER HIM HELPLESS
TO MAKE A STAND

BUT IT WAS
TO NO AVAIL
THE MAN HAD COURAGE
AND IT PREVAILED

HE LOOKED DEATH
STRAIGHT IN THE EYE
THE MAN WAS KILLED
BUT HE DID NOT DIE

A LESSON TO BE LEARNED

ONCE UPON A TIME
A LESSON WAS LEARNED
A LESSON
OF HIGH CONCERN

TAUGHT BY THE GREATEST TEACHER
OF ALL TIME
IT WAS THE LESSON
OF BEING IN A BIND

DEALING WITH
THE SITUATION AT HAND
THAT PERSON LEARNED
TO UNDERSTAND

THAT DEALING WITH
THE HARDSHIPS OF LIFE
BRINGS THE TRUTH
TO THE LIGHT

FOLLOW WHERE THE WIND BLOWS

ONCE UPON A TIME
THERE CAME A STRONG BREEZE
BLOWING A BIRDS' NEST
OUT OF A TREE

WHAT A TERRIBLE
BLOW IT WAS
FOR THE BIRD
IN SEARCH OF

THE BIRD DIDN'T HAVE
THE SENSE TO KNOW
FOLLOW WHERE
THE WIND BLOWS

AND SOMETIMES
NEITHER DO WE
UNTIL OUR NEST
IS BLOW OUT ITS' TREE

FORTUNATE FOR THE BIRD
NO EGGS WERE IN THE NEST
FORTUNATE FOR US
THERE'S NORTH, SOUTH, EAST AND WEST

FOR THE BIRD CAN ALWAYS
BUILD ANOTHER HOME
AND WE CAN FOLLOW
WHEREVER THE WIND BLOWS

A CASTLE MADE OF SAND

ONCE UPON A TIME
THERE WAS A CASTLE MADE OF SAND
SAID TO BE BUILT
BY A WISE MAN

SOME PEOPLE SAY
IT'S MILLIONS OF YEARS OLD
AND THAT ITS' SAND
IS MADE OF GOLD

PEOPLE CAME
FROM MILES AROUND
TO WHERE THIS CASTLE
COULD BE FOUND

IT STOOD IN THE SAND
BY THE SEA
UPON THE VERGE
OF REALITY

THE CASTLE HAS BEEN SEEN
THROUGHOUT THE AGES
BY VARIOUS PEOPLE
OF ALL GROUPS AND AGES

FOR SOME IT WAS A DREAM
A WISH, A HOPE
FOR SOME A FOOLS' PARADISE
WHERE THEY DON'T HAVE TO COPE

BUT THE ONE THING IN COMMON
THAT ALL PEOPLE SEE
IS THAT THE CASTLE
WAS NOT MEANT TO BE

LOST MIND

ONCE UPON A TIME
THIS PERSON LOST THEIR MIND
IT OPENED THEIR EYES
FOR THEY WERE BLIND

FOR THEY HAD LOST
THEIR MIND OF OLD
AND FOUND THE WAY
TO THEIR SOUL

THE END OF THE WORLD

ONCE UPON A TIME
THE WORLD CAVE IN
COLLAPSING INSIDE
AND FOLDING AT ALL ENDS

THERE WAS NOWHERE TO RUN
AND NOWHERE TO HIDE
THERE WAS NO WAY
TO SURVIVE

THE END OF THE WORLD
HAD COME
DEATH TOLL
ONE

THE SINGING OF A SONG

ONCE UPON A TIME
THERE WAS A SONG
EVERYONE JOINED IN
AND SANG ALONG

THEY ALL SANG
UNTIL THEIR HEARTS CONTENT
BUT FOR EVERYONE
THE SONG WAS NOT MEANT

IT BECAME EVIDENT
THE REASON WHY
WHEN IT CAME TIME
TO SAY GOOD-BYE

EVERYONE WENT
THEIR OWN WAY
BUT NOT WITH EVERYONE
DID THE SONG STAY

TO SING AND REJOICE
IS NOT ENOUGH
ONE HAS TO
BE IN TOUCH

IN THE NAME OF LOVE

ONCE UPON A TIME
IN THE NAME OF LOVE
THE GIFT OF LIFE
WAS GRANTED FROM ABOVE

FROM A TIME IMMORTAL
AND A PLACE DIVINE
THE LIGHT OF LOVE
HAS ALWAYS SHINED

THE PRECIOUS GIFT
OF LIFE IS HERE
SO THAT WE BY LOVE
CAN BE THERE

THE GREATEST ENEMY

ONCE UPON A TIME
A LONG TIME AGO
MAN BECAME
HIS GREATEST FOE

EVERYTHING HE
ENDEAVORED TO DO
LED TO
HIS OWN ABUSE

SO SELF-DESTRUCTIVE
IS THE NATURE OF MAN
THAT MAN IS UNABLE
TO UNDERSTAND

HE BELIEVES THE END
JUSTIFIES THE MEANS
THE CAUSE OF DEATH
OF MANY HUMAN BEINGS

EVEN IN
TIMES OF PEACE
MILLIONS DIE
IN THE STREETS

FOR MAN IS
TOO BLIND TO SEE
HE IS HIS
GREATEST ENEMY

ESCAPE FROM REALITY

ONCE UPON A TIME
IN AN EFFORT TO BE FREE
AN ESCAPE WAS MADE
FROM REALITY

REALITY IS DESIGNED
AS SUCH
TO ESCAPE
DOESN'T TAKE MUCH

WHAT A GOOD FEELING
IT WAS
TO BE AWAY FROM
FROM ALL THE FUSS

THIS IS LIFE
THE WAY IT SHOULD BE
SO MUCH PEACE
AND HARMONY

THIS IS WHERE
EVERYONE BELONGS
HOW COULD SOMETHING SO RIGHT
BE SO WRONG

INVISIBILITY

ONCE UPON A TIME
THERE WAS AN INVISIBLE MAN
WHO ROAMED ABOUT
THROUGHOUT THE LAND

BECAUSE HE COULD NOT
BE SEEN
HE SHIED AWAY
FROM HUMAN BEINGS

UNTIL HE ENCOUNTERED
ONE WHO WAS BLIND
THEY TALKED AND LAUGHED
AND HAD A GREAT TIME

THEY BECAME
THE BEST OF FRIENDS
BECAUSE THE BLIND MAN
SAW WITHIN

A MYSTERY

ONCE UPON A TIME
THERE WAS SAID TO BE
A MYSTICAL CITY
BENEATH THE SEA

ENHANCING THE PROBABLE DEPTH
OF MANKIND
PLACING IN REVERSE
THE HANDS OF TIME

WHO CAN SAY
IF IT WAS TRUE
IT'S A MYSTERY
TO ME AND YOU

LIKE ALL THINGS
BEFORE OUR TIME
IT REQUIRES
AN OPEN MIND

THE MASTER PLAN

ONCE UPON A TIME
I MET A WISE MAN
WHO EXPLAINED TO ME
"THE MASTER PLAN"

HE TOLD ME
THE ULTIMATE PURPOSE OF LIFE
IS TO BRING THE WORLD
INTO "THE LIGHT"

HE SPOKE OF PEOPLE
LIVING IN SIN
AND HOW THAT WORLD
WOULD COME TO AN END

HE SAID
IT WILL BE FULFILLED
ACCORDING TO
THE LORDS' WILL

THE "MASTER PLAN" HE SAID
WAS SOLEY DESIGNED
TO ELEVATE THE CONSCIOUSNESS
OF MANKIND

TO THE LEVEL
WHERE WE CAN SEE
GOD IS THE MASTER
OF OUR DESTINY

OASIS

ONCE UPON A TIME
IN NO MANS' LAND
AN OASIS WAS DISCOVERED
IN THE DESERT SAND

THE NOMAD LOOKED
WITH GREAT SURPRISE
HE COULDN'T BELIEVE
WHAT WAS BEFORE HIS EYES

HERE WAS THE MIRAGE
THAT SOME HAD SEEN
ONLY HERE IT WAS
AS THE REAL THING

BUT WHAT GOOD IS AN OASIS
TO A MAN
WHO DWELLS ONLY
IN THE DESERT SAND

NEVER STAYING IN ONE PLACE
TOO LONG
IN AN OASIS
HE DID NOT BELONG

THE TRUTH IN A LIE

ONCE UPON A TIME
I KNOW NOT WHY
TRUTH WAS OVERCOME
BY LIES

WHAT SHOULD BE
PLAIN TO SEE
REMAINS TO US
A MYSTERY

SUBMERGED IN THE DARKNESS
OF LIES
TRUTH STRUGGLES
TO SURVIVE

THE KING OF BEAST

ONCE UPON A TIME
IN THE JUNGLE DEEP
A FIGHT TOOK PLACE
FOR THE KING OF BEAST

A STRUGGLE ENSUED
UNTO DEATH
THE WINNER
WAS NOT THE BEST

HE DIDN'T WIN
FAIR AND SQUARE
HE WAS CLAD IN SAFARI
AND USED A SNARE

A KING OF BEAST
THAT HE WAS
ONE A MAN
SHOULD NOT BE PROUD OF

REALITY II

ONCE UPON A TIME
I CAME TO THE CONCLUSION
THAT I WAS LIVING
IN AN ILLUSION

REALITY SLAPPED ME
IN THE FACE
AND LET ME KNOW
I WAS OUT OF PLACE

IT HIT ME SO HARD
I FELL TO THE GROUND
MY WORLD COLLAPSED
ALL AROUND

I GOT UP SLOW
AND IN A DAZE
AND TRIED MY BEST
TO BE BRAVE

BUT WITH NO FOUNDATION
FOR ME TO STAND
ME AND MY WORLD
COLLAPSED AGAIN

THE ILLUSIONS SHATTERED
AND SO DID I
SOMEHOW I MANAGED
TO SURVIVE

BUT ON THE-OTHER-HAND
IT SET ME FREE
AND BROUGHT
ME TO REALITY

GRADUALLY MY LIFE
BEGAN TO CHANGE
AS REALITY BECAME
MORE INGRAINED

LIFE BECAME
MORE REAL TO ME
MY LIFE BECAME
A REALITY

NOW I HAVE
NO SELF-DOUBT
I KNOW AND LOVE
WHAT LIFE IS ABOUT

THE ONLY THING
I REGRET

IS THAT MY FRIENDS
HAVEN'T SEEN IT YET

BEING WITH THEM
IS NO LONGER A THRILL
BECAUSE FOR NOW ON
I'M KEEPING IT REAL

CHARACTER

ONCE UPON A TIME
I KNOW NOT WHEN
OR HOW THIS STORY
ACTUALLY BEGINS

BUT IT'S A STORY
THAT MUST BE TOLD
TO THE YOUNG
AND TO THE OLD

NEVER MIND THE SETTING
AND THE SPECIFIC SCENES
THE CHARACTER
IS THE IMPORTANT THING

THE CENTRAL THEME
OF EVERY CHAPTER
THIS IS A STORY
OF CHARACTER.

A GROWING TIME

ONCE UPON A TIME
IT WAS A TIME TO GROW
A TIME TO REAP
A TIME TO SOW

A TIME TO LEARN
A TIME TO TEACH
A TIME TO FIND
INNER PEACE

A TIME OF RIGHT
A TIME OF WRONG
A TIME TO CHOOSE
WHERE TO BELONG

A TIME OF FAITH
A TIME OF DESPAIR
A TIME FOR THE NEED
TO BE AWARE

A TIME OF HAPPINESS
A TIME OF PAIN
A TIME TO THINK
AND USE OUR BRAIN

A TIME TO BE BOLD
A TIME TO FEAR
A TIME TO LISTEN
WITH BOTH EARS

A TIME TO CRY
A TIME TO REJOICE
A TIME FOR US
TO MAKE A CHOICE

A TIME OF LOVE
A TIME OF HATE
A TIME TO LEARN
HOW TO RELATE

A TIME OF STABILITY
A TIME OF CHANGE
A TIME TO SEE
WHAT REMAINS

A TIME OF THE FUTURE
A TIME OF THE PAST
A TIME THAT WILL
ALWAYS LAST

FOR IT'S
A TIME TO GROW

A TIME TO REAP
A TIME TO SOW

A REVELATION

ONCE UPON A TIME
OUT OF THE CLEAR BLUE
A REVELATION
CAME THROUGH

AS A REVELATION
WOULD HAVE IT BE
THE TRUTH WAS NOW
PLAIN TO SEE

CONCEIVED IN THE FLASH
OF A MOMENT TIME
THAT TOOK YEARS
AND YEARS TO FIND

THE STANDING STILL OF TIME

ONCE UPON A TIME
TIME STOOD STILL
IT WAS ABSOLUTELY
UN-FOR-REAL

ALL PROGRESSION
CEASE TO BE
INTO A MOTIONLESS
STATE OF REALITY

NOTHING MOVED
NOT EVEN THE WIND
UNTIL TIME
RESUMED AGAIN

DURING THE MYSTERIOUS
BREAK IN TIME
SOME PEOPLE
LOSS THEIR MIND

AND THOSE WHO
REMAINED SANE
LIFE WOULD NEVER
BE THE SAME

COULD THIS EVER
HAPPEN AGAIN
WHEN TIME STOPS
AND STARTS AGAIN

ALTHOUGH WE DON'T
BELIEVE IT WILL
BEWARE OF DAYS
WHEN TIME STANDS STILL

ACCORDING TO ONES' VISION

ONCE UPON A TIME
AS FAR AS THE EYE COULD SEE
IT WAS THE WAY
IT HAD TO BE

BUT FOR THOSE WHO COULD
SEE BEYOND
IT WAS A WAY
FREE OF ALL BONDS

IT'S ACCORDING
TO ONES' VISION
THAT GIVES THE WORLD
ITS' DIMENSION

A VICTIM OF SELF

ONCE UPON A TIME
A MAN FELL VICTIM
DUE TO AN INABILITY
TO LISTEN

THE MAN COULD NOT
BE TOLD A THING
ALWAYS TALKING
WHEN HE SHOULD BE LISTENING

SO SELF-CENTERED
WAS HE
OTHERS POINT OF VIEW
HE FAILED TO SEE

HE WENT
THROUGH LIFE
ALWAYS THINKING
HE WAS RIGHT

CAUGHT UP
IN HIS OWN SYSTEM
OF WHICH
HE FELL VICTIM

THE CHURCH OF THE LORD

ONCE UPON A TIME
THERE WAS A CHURCH
IT WAS THE ATTAINMENT
OF THE ULTIMATE SEARCH

LOCATED UPON
THE THRESHOLD OF TIME
IN THE TEMPLE
OF THE UNIVERSAL MIND

THERE IT WAS
THE CHURCH COULD BE FOUND
STANDING UPON
THE HIGHEST GROUND

THERE THE LORD
WELCOMED ALL
WITH THE ABILITY
TO ANSWER HIS CALL

FOR SEARCHERS
IN THE WORLD TODAY
THAT CHURCH
IS TOO FAR AWAY

SO THE LORD
WILL COME TO THEM
TO TAKE THEM BACK
WITH HIM

FAILURE

ONCE UPON A TIME
THERE WAS A WELL
INTO WHICH
A PERSON FELL

DOWN, DOWN
DOWN THEY WENT
DOWN INTO
A BOTTOMLESS PIT

WITH THE BOTTOM
NOWHERE IN SIGHT
THEY REACHED ROCK BOTTOM
IN THEIR LIFE

THEY FAIL AGAIN
AGAIN AND AGAIN
TO THEIR FAILURE
THERE WAS NO END

LIKE FALLING INTO A DEEP WELL
IS THE WAY IT FELT
VOID OF ALL HOPE
VOID OF ALL HELP

MY PEOPLE WERE ONCE FREE

ONCE UPON A TIME
MY PEOPLE WERE FREE
UNTIL THE BONDAGE
OF SLAVERY

TAKEN TO A LAND
THOUSANDS OF MILES AWAY
MY PEOPLE WERE FORCED
TO BECOME SLAVES

STRIPPED OF THEIR PRIDE
AND PUT TO SHAME
USED AND ABUSED
FOR PROFIT AND GAIN

ONLY A STRONG WILL
TO STAY ALIVE
ENABLED MY PEOPLE
TO SURVIVE

AFTER MANY YEARS OF OPPRESSION
WORD CAME DOWN
SLAVERY WAS NOT A CONCEPT
UPON WHICH THE LAND WAS FOUND

SO MY PEOPLE WERE ORDERED
TO BE SET FREE
IN THIS LAND
OF SWEET LIBERTY

BUT AS A RESULT
OF BEING IN THIS PLACE
MY PEOPLE HAD BECOME
A LOST RACE

HOW CAN MY PEOPLE
EVER AGAIN BE FREE
WHEN THEY HAVE LOST
THEIR IDENTITY

A DREAM COME TRUE

ONCE UPON A TIME
A DREAM CAME TRUE
A DREAM THAT HAD TO
BE PURSUED

DREAMS OF THIS NATURE
DON'T OCCUR IN SLEEP
WE MUST BE WIDE AWAKE
STANDING ON OUR OWN TWO FEET

BUT AS A DREAM
WOULD HAVE IT BE
IT WAS BEYOND THE NORM
OF REALITY

A VISION CONCEIVED
WITHIN THE MIND
TAKING ITS' PLACE
IN THE ANNALS OF TIME

A GIFT TO BELIEVE IN

ONCE UPON A TIME
THERE WAS A GIFTED CHILD
WHO CAME INTO THE WORLD
SPIRITUALLY ENDOWED

THE CHILD KNEW
WITHOUT BEING TAUGHT
AND PERCEIVED
WHAT OTHERS COULD NOT

WHEN THE CHILD WAS ASK
HOW COULD THIS BE
THE CHILD REPLIED
IT'S A MYSTERY

THE GIFT IS NOT MINES
FOR ME TO REASON
THE GIFT IS MINES
FOR ME TO BELIEVE IN

THE FIRST DAY OF SPRING

ONCE UPON A TIME
ON THE FIRST DAY OF SPRING
IT WAS SAID TO BE
THE MOST BEAUTIFUL THING

THE SKY WAS
CRYSTAL CLEAR BLUE
CASTING A REFLECTION
OF ALL THINGS NEW

THE SUN WAS SO BRIGHT
ITS' RAYS SO WARM
PEOPLE FELT LIKE
THEY WERE REBORN

THE GENTLENESS OF THE BREEZE
IN THE AIR
GAVE A TOUCH OF DIVINENESS
TO THE ATMOSPHERE

THE BIRDS SANG
SUCH WONDERFUL TUNES
IT MADE MARCH
SEEM LIKE JUNE

ABSENT-MINDEDNESS

ONCE UPON A TIME
THERE WAS A ABSENT-MINDED KING
THE LAME BRAIN
COULDN'T REMEMBER A THING

THERE WAS NOTHING UNUSUAL
ABOUT THAT
FOR NOBODY IN THE KINGDOM
COULD REMEMBER A FACT

YET LIFE WENT ON
AS STRANGE AS IT MAY SEEM
THEN THEY ALL FORGOT
WHO WAS THE KING

THIS PLACED THE KING
ON THE SPOT
AND HE TOO
HAD FORGOT

SO IN THE PLACE OF THE KING
"FORGETFULNESS" REIGNED
AS RIGHTFUL RULER
OVER THE KINGDOM OF LAME BRAINS

LOVE WAS SO GREAT

ONCE UPON A TIME
LOVE WAS SO GREAT
THERE WAS NO SUCH THING
AS HATE

SO POWERFUL
WAS THE FORCE OF LOVE
IT WAS THE ONLY
FORCE THERE WAS

UNTIL MATERIALISM
CAME INTO BEING
WITH ALL ITS'
SUPERFICIAL THINGS

IT DISTORTED
THE CONCEPT OF LOVE
AND ALL THAT LOVE
WAS MADE OF

WHAT WE KNOW
AS LOVE TODAY
IS NOT THE GREATNESS
OF THE PURITY OF LOVES' WAY

ALL THINGS REVEALED

ONCE UPON A TIME
NO ONE KNEW WHY
THE SUN ROSE
AND SET IN THE SKY

ONCE A MYSTERY
BUT NOT ANYMORE
LIKEWISE WE SHALL DISCOVER
ALL THAT WE'RE SEARCHING FOR

FOR ALL THINGS
ARE REVEALED IN TIME
UPON ALL THINGS
THE SUN SHALL SHINE

WORK & PLAY

ONCE UPON A TIME
THE PEOPLE USE TO SAY
LIFE IS ALL WORK
AND NO PLAY

AS IT WAS
WAY BACK THEN
BUT IT SHALL NEVER
BE AGAIN

WORKING PEOPLE
NOW UNDERSTAND
WORK AND PLAY
GO HAND IN HAND

A CITY OF GLASS

ONCE UPON A TIME
THERE WAS A CITY OF GLASS
ITS' MAGNIFICENCE
WAS UNSURPASSED

THE CITY WAS
A BREATH OF VISION
TRANSPARENT FIGURES
OF MULTIPLE DIMENSIONS

IN EVERY RESPECT
A HEAVENLY SHRINE
THOUSANDS OF YEARS
AHEAD OF ITS' TIME

A GREAT LOOKING GLASS
FOR THE WORLD TO SEE
THE THIN LINE
SEPARATING REALITY

IT COMES TO PASS

ONCE UPON A TIME
IT CAME TO PASS
BUT LIKE ALL THINGS
IT DID NOT LAST

ALTHOUGH IT SHOULD
LAST FOREVER
OVER TIME
GET BETTER AND BETTER

BUT NO ONE THING
IS TRULY MEANT TO BE
NOTHING IN ITSELF
IS COMPLETE

IT'S EVERYTHING
AS A WHOLE
THAT HAS BEEN
FROM TIMES OF OLD

IT IS EVERYTHING
THAT HAS BEEN
THAT COMES TO PASS
AGAIN AND AGAIN

DESTINY

ONCE UPON A TIME
THE WORLD USE TO BE
A PLACE
OF UNKNOWN DESTINY

THEN THE WORLD
BEGAN TO TAKE SHAPE
WITH THE CREATION
OF THE HUMAN RACE

DARKNESS THEN
GAVE WAY TO LIGHT
REVEALING THE PURPOSE
AND DESTINY OF LIFE

THE WORLD
BECAME REVOLUTIONIZED
CONSTANTLY CHANGING
BEING REVISED

NO LONGER IS THE WORLD
WHAT IT USE TO BE
IT'S A WORLD
FULFILLING ITS' DESTINY

A LITTLE GIRL ALL GROWN UP

ONCE UPON A TIME
A LITTLE GIRL ENVISIONED
HOW LITTLE GIRLS GROW UP
AND BECOME WOMEN

IT ALL BEGAN
WHILE PLAYING HOUSE
THAT SHE ENVISIONED
WHAT A WOMAN WAS ABOUT

HER BABY DOLLS
WERE NOT JUST A GAME
THEY WERE HER BABIES
SHE GAVE THEM NAMES

SHE CARED FOR THEM
LIKE A GOOD MOTHER
AND LOOK FORWARD TO THE DAY
SHE WOULD FIND HER LOVER

WHEN SHE MET THE BOY
WHO WOULD BE THE FATHER
SHE WAS PREPARED
FOR HER SON OR DAUGHTER

ONE THING LED
TO ANOTHER
AND SHE BECAME
A REAL MOTHER

A WORK OF ART

ONCE UPON A TIME
A ARTIST PAINTED A SCENE
IT WAS EXACTLY LIKE
THE REAL THING

THE CLOUDS SEEM TO MOVE
IN THE BLUE SKY
ABOVE THE MOUNTAIN TOPS
EVER SO HIGH

THE WIND SEEM TO BLOW
THROUGH THE TREES
BRANCHES SWAYING
IN THE BREEZE

BUT IT ALL CAME
STRAIGHT FROM THE HEART
MANIFESTING AS
A WORK OF ART

CREATIVITY
AT THE SOURCE
GENERATING
NATURES' FORCE

A GIFT

ONCE UPON A TIME
AT THE GIVING OF A GIFT
PRESENT WAS THE FEELING
OF TRUE HAPPINESS

THE GIFT
WAS ACTUALLY A TOKEN
FOR WORDS
THAT COULD NOT BE SPOKEN

A DREAM

ONCE UPON A TIME
THIS PERSON HAD A DREAM
THAT CHANGED THEIR LIFE
OR SO IT SEEMED

THAT DREAM BECAME
THEIR GUIDING LIGHT
IT GAVE DIRECTION
TO HIS LIFE

THE ULTIMATE GOAL
OF WHAT THEY WANTED TO BE
WAS TO MAKE THEIR DREAM
A REALITY

WHILE EMBARKED
ON THIS PATH IN LIFE
NOTHING SEEMED
TO BE MORE RIGHT

UNTIL THE DAY
THEIR DREAM CAME TRUE
AND THEY REALIZED IT WASN'T
WHAT THEY WANTED TO DO

TIMES SUCH AS THIS

ONCE UPON A TIME
A MAN SOUGHT TO FIND
A WAY TO STOP
THE HANDS OF TIME

HE FIGURED HE COULD MAKE
TIME STAND STILL
BY ALTERING WHAT WAS KNOWN
TO BE REAL

SINCE TIME IS THE ESSENCE
OF ALL THINGS
TIME COULD BE STOPPED
OR SO IT SEEMED

SO HE WENT ABOUT CHANGING
THE WAY THINGS WERE
UNTIL ONE DAY
IT FINALLY OCCURRED

TIME CAME
TO A SCREECHING HALT
BUT WITH
NEGATIVE RESULTS

HE WAS ABLE TO STOP
THE HANDS OF TIME
AT THE EXPENSE
OF MANKIND

FOR THE TIME
THAT CEASE TO BE
WAS THE DESTRUCTION
OF REALITY

YOU SEE THIS MAN
HE WAS NO SAINT
HE SOUGHT CONTROL OF
A WORLD THAT AIN'T

EVERY SO OFTEN
SUCH A PERSON COMES ALONG
POKING HIS NOSE
WHERE IT DON'T BELONG

ATTEMPTING TO BE
LIKE NO OTHER
CAUSING CATASTROPHIES
ONE RIGHT AFTER ANOTHER

TRUTH

ONCE UPON A TIME
LONG BEFORE YOU AND I
TRUTH WAS BORN
NEVER TO DIE

BORN OF THE ESSENCE
OF WHAT WAS TO BE
TRUTH LAID CLAIM
UPON YOU AND ME

BY ESTABLISHMENT OF THE LAW
AND ORDER OF LIFE
TRUTH HOLDS US RESPONSIBLE
TO DO WHAT'S RIGHT

AS WE SOW
SO SHALL WE REAP
FOR BY THE TRUTH
WE EARN OUR KEEP

TRUTH CAN LIFT YOU UP
OR BREAK YOU DOWN
MOVE YOU FORWARD
OR TURN YOU AROUND

IT ALL DEPENDS
UPON YOU
SO TO YOURSELF
ALWAYS BE TRUE

WORDS GREATER THAN ACTION

ONCE UPON A TIME
AS I CONCUR
ACTION DOES NOT ALWAYS SPEAK
LOUDER THAN WORDS

THERE ARE TIMES
WHEN WORDS CAN SAY
WHAT ACTION
COULD NEVER CONVEY

LIKE A MOTHERS' WORDS
TO HER DAUGHTER
LIKE THE WORDS TO A SON
FROM HIS FATHER

LIKE THE WORDS
BETWEEN SISTER AND BROTHER
LIKE THE WORDS
BETWEEN FATHER AND MOTHER

WHEN THESE WORDS
GO UNSAID
ALL OTHER ACTIONS
MAY JUST WELL BE DEAD

A DAY WITHOUT THE SUN

ONCE UPON A TIME
THE SUN DID NOT RISE
THE PEOPLE THOUGHT
THEY WOULD SURELY DIE

SUBMERGED IN DARKNESS
AND SCARED TO DEATH
THEY WONDERED HOW MUCH TIME
THEY HAD LEFT

NOONTIME CAME
AND STILL NO SUN
THEY THOUGHT FOR SURE
THE END OF THE WORLD HAD COME

BY EVENING TIME
THEY WERE REALLY SCARED
ALL WERE PRAYING
FOR THEIR LIVES TO BE SPARED

AS THEY PRAYED
THE SUN BEGAN TO RISE
THE PEOPLE BECAME HOPEFUL
THEY WOULD SURVIVE

THEY WERE SO HAPPY
TO SEE THE LIGHT
THEY FORGOT ALL ABOUT
IT WAS SUPPOSE TO NIGHT

WHEN IT DAWNED ON THEM
THEY DIDN'T SEEM TO CARE
ALL THAT MATTERED
WAS THAT THE SUN WAS THERE

AND YOU KNOW SOMETHING
THEY WERE RIGHT
BECAUSE THE MOST IMPORTANT THING
IS THE SUNS' LIGHT

A CRAZY MAN & A FOOL

ONCE UPON A TIME
THERE WAS A CRAZY MAN AND A FOOL
NEITHER ONE
HAD THE SENSE OF A MULE

THE CRAZY MAN CARRIED ON
IN SUCH A WAY
HE WAS CERTIFIED
AND PUT AWAY

THE FOOL AVOIDED
SUCH A FATE
KNOWING WHEN
AND WHEN NOT TO RELATE

THE DIFFERENCE
BETWEEN THE TWO
IS ONE IS FALSE
THE OTHER IS TRUE

THE FOOL IS AWARE
OF THE WAY HE ACTS
BUT THE CRAZY MAN
HAS LOST ALL TRACK

ALTHOUGH NEITHER ONE
IS IN THEIR RIGHT MIND
I'D CHOOSE A CRAZY MAN
OVER A FOOL ANYTIME

FOR A PERSON TO KNOWINGLY ACT
IN A INSANE WAY
THAT'S THE ONE
WHO SHOULD BE PUT AWAY

THE GREATNESS

ONCE UPON A TIME
A GREATNESS COULD BE SEEN
A GREATNESS THAT EXISTED
IN EVERYTHING

LIKE RAYS OF LIGHT
SHINNING VERY BRIGHT
SO WAS THE QUALITY
OF ALL LIFE

NOW JUST
A FLICKER REMAINS
OF THE GREATNESS
OF LIFES' FLAME

THOUGH STILL OUTSTANDING
AS IT MAY BE
THE GREATNESS
WE FAIL TO SEE

A PREDICTION FOR EVERY AGE

ONCE UPON A TIME
A PREDICTION WAS MADE
THAT WOULD OCCUR
IN EVERY AGE

IT WAS PREDICTED
THAT THERE WOULD BE
NO END TO THE FULFILLMENT
OF THIS PROPHECY

THAT EACH AGE
WOULD BRING ABOUT
THINGS MANKIND WOULD BE
BETTER OFF WITHOUT

TWO PEOPLE

ONCE UPON A TIME
TWO PEOPLE GOT TOGETHER
IN WHAT WAS SUPPOSE TO
BE FOREVER

HOWEVER IT WASN'T
MEANT TO BE
SO THEY SET
EACH OTHER FREE

WHEN TWO PEOPLE
NO LONGER SEE EYE TO EYE
IT'S BETTER FOR THEM
TO SAY GOOD-BYE

IN THE HEAT OF THE DAY

ONCE UPON A TIME
IN THE HEAT
UNDER A TREE
IN THE SHADE

FROM THE HEAT
HE WAS SAVED
THERE HE WISHED
HE COULD STAY

HOPING HE WOULD
HAVE HIS WAY
HE THOUGHT HE WOULD
HAVE IT MADE

SHELTERED FROM
THE SUNS' RAYS
TO THE TREE
HE GAVE PRAISE

BUT THE TREE
MAY JUST WELL BEEN ABLAZE
FOR THAT MAN
WAS A SLAVE

STRANGE NOTIONS

ONCE UPON A TIME
EVERYONE HAD STRANGE NOTIONS
ABOUT EVERYTHING
FROM SUPERSTITION TO MAGIC POTIONS

ALL BUT FORGOTTEN
ARE THEY TODAY
BUT THE STRANGE NOTIONS
HAVE NOT GONE AWAY

FOR AS STRANGE
AS IT MAY SEEM
SOME PEOPLE ARE STILL DOING
THE SAME OLD THING

THE MYSTERY OF THE WORLD

ONCE UPON A TIME
ALL MYSTERIES WERE REVEALED
THEN THE WORLD CHANGED
AND THEY BECAME CONCEALED

DUE TO THE CHANGE
IN REALITY
THE WORLD
BECAME A MYSTERY

REVEALING ITS' SECRETS
ONLY TO THE WISE
WHO LOOK BEYOND
THE VISION OF THEIR EYES

THAT'S WHAT THE CHANGE
WAS ALL ABOUT
TO KEEP WISDOM WITHIN
AND FALSEHOOD OUT

A KINGS' WEALTH

ONCE UPON A TIME
THERE WAS A WEALTHY KING
MONEY AND POWER
WAS THE ULTIMATE THING

HIS KINGDOM EXPANDED
TO THE ENDS OF THE EARTH
NOT EVEN HE KNEW
HOW MUCH HE WAS WORTH

HE ACHIEVED
WHAT NO ONE ELSE HAD EVER DONE
HE WAS THE GREATEST OF ALL KINGS
UNDER THE SUN

YET HE STILL WANTED
TO HAVE MORE
SO HE SOUGHT AFTER
THE KINGDOM OF THE LORD

BUT ALL THE KINGS WEALTH
COULD NOT BUY
A PLACE FOR THE KING
IN THE SKY

CHRISTMAS WITHOUT SANTA

ONCE UPON A TIME
ONE CHRISTMAS DAY
SOMEONE STOLE
SANTAS' SLEIGH

SANTA REPORTED IT
TO THE POLICE
WHO ONLY HAD HOURS
TO TRACK DOWN THE THIEF

THEY FOLLOWED THE TRACKS
LEFT IN THE SNOW
TO A PLACE
WHERE NO MAN COULD GO

THE POLICE WERE BAFFLED
DIDN'T KNOW WHAT TO DO
THEIR SEARCH HAD FAILED
TO TURN A CLUE

SO THEY CALLED IN
THE FBI
WITH VERY LITTLE TIME LEFT
TO FIND THE GUY

THEY TOO WERE BAFFLED
BY THE TRACKS
AND DECIDED
THEY'D HAVE TO TURN BACK

BUT THEN
JUST IN THE NICK OF TIME
AN IDEA CAME
INTO SANTAS' MIND

LETS' MAKE THIS CHRISTMAS
A DAY OF THE LORD
AND CELEBRATE IT
LIKE IT WAS BEFORE

MAYBE THE THEFT
WAS AN ACT OF GOD
THAT WOULD EXPLAIN
THE TRACKS BEING SO ODD

THE CHILDREN
WILL JUST HAVE TO UNDERSTAND
THAT AFTER ALL
I'M JUST A MAN

QUESTIONS IN THE MIND

ONCE UPON A TIME
A YOUNGSTER SET OUT TO FIND
ANSWERS TO THE QUESTIONS
IN HIS MIND

HIS PARENTS KNEW NOT
WHAT TO SAY
FROM HIS PARENTS
HE WENT ASTRAY

OUT INTO THE WORLD
HE WENT
HAVING NO IDEA
WHAT IT MEANT

EXPERIENCE BEING THE TEACHER
THAT IT IS
ANSWERED HIS QUESTIONS
AND NOW HE'S DEAD

THE WORLD IS
A BAD PLACE TO FIND
ANSWERS TO THE QUESTIONS
IN A YOUNGSTERS' MIND

NOTHING IS IMPOSSIBLE

ONCE UPON A TIME
MERMAIDS LIVED IN THE SEA
WHICH SOME PEOPLE
FIND HARD TO BELIEVE

MY BELIEF
IS THIS
WHETHER OR NOT
IT BE A MYTH

KNOWING THE UNIVERSE
ITS' VASTNESS AND AGE
NOTHING IS IMPOSSIBLE
NOT EVEN A MERMAID

LIFE IS NOT IN VAIN

ONCE UPON A TIME
IT BECAME OF ESSENCE
IN THE PAST
TO THE PRESENT

THAT IT NOT
BE IN VAIN
WHAT COULD NOT
REMAIN THE SAME

SO WITHIN
THE PROCESS OF TIME
THE LORD LET
HIS LIGHT SHINE

GIVING LIFE
REASON TO BE
BY THE PURPOSE
OF OUR DESTINY

FEARLESS

ONCE UPON A TIME
IN A STATE OF FEAR
ON THE BRINK
OF UTTER DESPAIR

PEACE OF MIND
WAS DISCOVERED THERE
LIFTING THE BURDEN
OF ALL CARES

IT'S WHEN ONE SUFFERS
THEIR GREATEST DESPAIR
THAT THEY ARE ABLE
TO ABANDON FEAR

FOR AT THAT POINT
IT BECOMES CLEAR
THERE IS NO REASON
TO LIVE IN FEAR

CELEBRATED HEROES

ONCE UPON A TIME
NOT SO LONG AGO
ONLY MEN
WERE CELEBRATED HEROES

NOW WOMEN
ARE CELEBRATED TOO
WOMEN ARE FINALLY
GETTING THEIR DUE

WOMEN HAVE COME
FROM FAR BEHIND
IT'S THE GREATEST CHANGE
SINCE THE BEGINNING OF TIME

LOVE LOST

ONCE UPON A TIME
NOTHING WAS MORE TRUE
THAN THE LOVE
I HAVE FOR YOU

IT'S STRANGE HOW THINGS CHANGE
WITH TIME
I THOUGHT YOU WOULD ALWAYS
BE MINE

NOW YOU ARE
NO LONGER HERE
ALL THAT'S LEFT
ARE YESTER-YEARS

WHAT GOOD ARE THEY
TO ME
WITHOUT THE LOVE
THAT USE TO BE

ANGELS IN DISGUISE

ONCE UPON A TIME
ANGELS APPEARED
TO THOSE WHOM GOD
LOVED SO DEAR

ALTHOUGH NOT AN ANGEL
IN THE CONVENTIONAL SENSE
THERE WAS NO DOUBT
THEY WERE HEAVEN SENT

PEOPLE OFTEN
COME INTO PLAY
TO BESTOW GODS' BLESSINGS
IN SUCH A WAY

DREAMS AND SIMPLE THINGS

ONCE UPON A TIME
LIFE WAS FILLED WITH DREAMS
AND PEOPLE CHERISHED
THE SIMPLE THINGS

THAT QUALITY OF LIFE
IS RARE TODAY
SIMPLICITY HAS ALL BUT
FADED AWAY

DREAMS THAT WERE ONCE
SHARED BY MANY
MOST CEASE TO BE
THERE HARDLY ANY

WHAT HAPPENED TO
THE AMERICAN DREAM
AND ALL THE LITTLE
SIMPLE THINGS

IS IT THAT
THE WORLD HAS CHANGED
OR ARE THE PEOPLE
NOT THE SAME

ONLY YOU KNOW
THE REASON WHY
FOR THE STANDARDS
YOU ARE LIVING BY

HAPPINESS

ONCE UPON A TIME
A WISH WAS MADE
THAT LIFE COULD HAVE
ALL HAPPY DAYS

SOMETIMES HAPPY
SOMETIMES SAD
IT'S A WISH
WE ALL HAVE

HAPPINESS IS THE PURSUIT
OF THE SOUL
BEGINNING IN YOUTH
AND PURSUED UNTIL OLD

HAPPINESS IS
WHAT MAKES LIFE WORTH LIVING
AND IN CONCLUSION
ALL THINGS FORGIVEN

STRANGE BUT TRUE

ONCE UPON A TIME
A STRANGE THING OCCURRED
WITHIN THE QUESTION
OF A FEW WORDS

AT FIRST IT DIDN'T
MAKE ANY SENSE
WHAT THE QUESTION
ACTUALLY MEANT

UNTIL IT WAS GIVEN
SOME THOUGHT
AND DISCOVERED THEMSELF
THEY KNOW NOT

YOUR NAME, YOUR SEX
THE THINGS YOU DO
DOESN'T ANSWER THE QUESTION
WHO ARE YOU
STRANGE BUT TRUE

THE SURFACE OF THINGS

ONCE UPON A TIME
IT WAS WELL KNOWN FACT
THE SHAPE OF EARTH
WAS FLAT

BY THE JUDGMENT
OF THE SURFACE OF THINGS
THAT'S THE WAY
EARTH SEEMED

TO LOOK AND SEE
IS NOT ENOUGH
BECAUSE THE SURFACE
IS A COVER UP

ALTHOUGH IT'S NOT
MEANT TO BE
THE SURFACE
HIDES REALITY

WE MUST BE WISE
IN ORDER TO KNOW
WHAT OUR EYES SEE
IS NOT ALWAYS SO

THE BEAST AND THE MEEK

ONCE UPON A TIME
IN A LAND OF BEAST
THE LAND WAS INHERITED
BY THE MEEK

THE END OF ALL THE BEAST
IN THE LAND
WAS COMPLETE
WITH THE EXTINCTION OF MAN

WITH ALL THINGS
BEING COMPLETE
THE MEEK PREVAILED
OVER THE BEAST

ACCORDING TO THE LAW
OF THE ORDER OF LIFE
THE MEEK LAID CLAIM
TO THEIR BIRTHRIGHT

A TIME OF CHANGE

ONCE UPON A TIME
THERE CAME A CHANGE
FROM THAT DAY FORTH
NOTHING REMAINED THE SAME

THE CHANGE CAME ABOUT
IN A NATURAL WAY
WHEN NIGHT
FIRST BECAME DAY

SETTING IN MOTION
THE CYCLE THAT WOULD BE
THE EVOLUTIONARY FORCE
OF ETERNITY

THE NAME OF THAT CHANGE
BECAME KNOWN AS TIME
THE RELEVANT FACTOR
OF THE UNIVERSE AND MANKIND

LIFE

ONCE UPON A TIME
A TURN OF EVENTS
REVEALED WHAT LIFE
TRULY MEANT

THOSE INVOLVED
WERE ABLE TO SEE
THEY WERE NOT IN CONTROL
OF THEIR DESTINY

WE ALL EXIST
AS HUMAN BEINGS
LIVING WITHIN
THE STRUCTURE OF THINGS

A WISE MAN

ONCE UPON A TIME
IN A FORBIDDEN LAND
THERE LIVED
A WISE MAN

HE LIVED THERE
AS A MATTER OF CHOICE
ALTHOUGH IT WAS NOT
A PLACE OF REJOICE

FOR IT WAS THERE
THAT HE SHOULD BE
TO BE OF HELP
TO THOSE IN NEED

HAPPINESS II

ONCE UPON A TIME
THE WORLD WAS TO BE
A PLACE WHERE ALL PEOPLE
WOULD BE HAPPY

THOSE WHO ARE HAPPY
HAVE TRULY BEEN BLESSED
WHILE SOME OTHERS
COULD CARE LESS

WHAT SOME PEOPLE CALL
HAVING FUN
I WOULDN'T WISH
UPON ANYONE

BY TAKING PLEASURE
IN DOING WRONG THINGS
WE'RE DESTROYING OUR LIVES
AS HUMAN BEINGS

SUCH A WORLD
WAS NOT MEANT TO BE
BUT SOME HAVE MADE IT
A REALITY

WE WOULD LIKE TO BE HAPPY
ALL THE TIME
BUT HAPPINESS
IS HARD TO FIND

UNLESS WE START LOOKING
IN THE RIGHT PLACE
HAPPINESS WILL CONTINUE TO HAVE
A FROWN UPON ITS' FACE

PEACE & HARMONY

ONCE UPON A TIME
THE WORLD USE TO BE
A PLACE OF PEACE
AND HARMONY

ALL PEOPLE
SISTERS AND BROTHERS
LIVING IN ACCORD
WITH ANOTHER

INDIVIDUAL ACTS
AND INDIVIDUAL DEEDS
SERVED THE PURPOSE
OF EVERYONES NEEDS

NOTHING WAS EVER
DONE IN VAIN
ALL WAS DONE
IN THE LORDS NAME

ACCORDING TO THE SPIRIT
ALL THINGS WERE
ALL THINGS HOLY
WERE OBSERVED

WHENEVER IN DOUBT
AS TO WHAT SHOULD BE
LOOK FOR PEACE
AND HARMONY

A BEAUTIFUL GIRL

ONCE UPON A TIME
THERE LIVED A BEAUTIFUL GIRL
KNOWN FOR HER BEAUTY
THROUGHOUT THE WORLD

HER BEAUTY BROUGHT HER
FORTUNE AND FAME
IT ALSO BROUGHT HER
A FEELING OF SHAME

BEING ADMIRED
FOR HER LOOKS
SHE HADN'T LEARN
TO CLEAN AND COOK

WITHOUT KNOWLEDGE
OF THE THINGS WOMEN DO
SHE REALIZED HER BEAUTY
WAS WORTHLESS TOO

SO SHE LEARNED
TO DO THOSE THINGS
AND FOUND THE LOVE
THAT BEAUTY CAN BRING

HER BEAUTY SURPASSED
A THING OF WEALTH
AND SHE WENT ON
TO FULFILL HERSELF

FAITH

ONCE UPON A TIME
A MAN FELL FROM GRACE
CAUSED BY
A LOSS OF FAITH

HE DIDN'T
REALIZE WHAT TOOK PLACE
BECAUSE THE TRUTH
HE REFUSED TO FACE

TO LOSE FAITH IN ANYTHING
THAT YOU BELIEVE
CAN BRING YOU DOWN
TO YOUR KNEES

THAT IS WHEN IT'S TIME
TO PRAY
HAVE FAITH IN GOD
IT'S THE ONLY WAY

THE CHILD WITHIN US ALL

ONCE UPON A TIME
THERE WAS A LITTLE CHILD
WHO HAD NO FRIENDS
AND HAD NO TOYS

THE CHILD WAS SAD
AS THE CHILD COULD BE
BECAUSE THE CHILD
WAS VERY LONELY

THEN ONE NIGHT
THE CHILD HAD A DREAM
WITH LOTS OF FRIENDS
AND TOYS AND THINGS

BUT WHEN THE CHILD AWOKE
THEY WERE NOT THERE
AND THE CHILDS' EYES
BECAME FILLED WITH TEARS

THEN A VOICE SAID
DRY YOUR EYES
YOU ARE NOT ALONE
I AM BY YOUR SIDE

THE CHILD WONDERED
WHO COULD IT BE
SHE DRIED HER EYES
SO SHE COULD SEE

BUT SHE SAW NO ONE
FOR NO ONE WAS THERE
YET SHE FELT BETTER
BECAUSE SHE HAD DRIED HER TEARS

SHE WAITED FOR THE VOICE
TO SPEAK AGAIN
THE VOICE SPOKE AND SAID
I AM YOUR FRIEND

THEY PLAYED AND PLAYED
AND SHE HAD A LOT OF FUN
YET THE VOICE THAT SPOKE
WAS REALLY NO ONE

IF YOU LISTEN VERY CLOSELY
YOU CAN HEAR IT TOO
FOR THAT SAME VOICE
IS WITHIN ME AND YOU

THERE USE TO BE

ONCE UPON A TIME
THERE WAS SAID TO BE
WONDERS BEYOND
WHAT THE EYE COULD SEE

TALES OF GODS AND GODDESSES
AND MAGICAL POWER
CAN BE HEARD
IN OLD TALES OF OURS

BUT THEN ONE SAYS
HOW CAN THIS BE
THAT SUCH THINGS
WERE EVER REALITY

BUT THEN WHO WOULD EXPECT
ANYONE TO BELIEVE
SUCH THINGS THE MIND
CAN NOT PERCEIVE

THE GREATEST SHOW

ONCE UPON A TIME
A SHOW WENT DOWN
INCLUDING ALL
THE BIGGEST STARS AROUND

BILLED AS THE GREATEST
SHOW EVER
TOO BAD IT COULDN'T
LAST FOREVER

FOR WHEN THE SHOW
WAS OVER AND DONE
SO TOO
WAS ALL THE FUN

ALTHOUGH THEY HAD MORE FUN
THAN EVER BEFORE
THERE WAS NO GREATER FUN
TO LOOK TOWARD

THAT'S WHY THE BEST THINGS
ARE BEST SAVED FOR LAST
OR THEY JUST BECOME
A THING OF THE PAST

AND ALL FUTURE DAYS
WILL BE
AN ATTEMPT TO DO
WHATS BEEN ACHIEVED

DEAD END

ONCE UPON A TIME
THERE WAS A DEAD END STREET
WHERE ALL FAILURES
ARE DESTINED TO MEET

THEY CAME FROM
ALL WALKS OF LIFE
MISSING THE TURN
TO THE RIGHT

CLAIMING ALL SORTS OF REASONS
FOR MISSING THE TURN
BUT THE TRUTH IS
SOME PEOPLE WILL NEVER LEARN

IF YOU TAKE A TURN
FOR THE WORST
IT'S BEST TO PUT IT
IN REVERSE

RATHER THAN PROCEED
JUST TO FIND
YOURSELF AT
THE END OF THE LINE

THE CREATOR

ONCE UPON A TIME
IN THE MIDST OF A STORM
A BEAUTIFUL NEW WORLD
WAS BORN

THE STORM WAS PERFECT
FOR THE SEED TO GROW
ALTHOUGH THE STORM
WAS ITS' VERY FOE

OUT OF ADVERSITY
GOOD THINGS MAY COME FORTH
BECAUSE GOD IS CREATOR
OF EVERY SOURCE

BLESSED

ONCE UPON A TIME
IN A LAND OF PLENTY
BLESSINGS WERE BESTOWED
UPON MANY

BUT FAILURE
TO SEE
THE BLESSINGS
THAT BE

THEY PROSPERED
IN ALL THINGS
BUT BLESSINGS
IT DID NOT BRING

FOR TO BE BLESSED
IT MUST BE KNOWN
WE ARE REAPING
WHAT GOD HAS SOWN

BY ACKNOWLEDGING GOD
IN ALL WE DO
IT BECOMES A BLESSING
UNTO YOU

A HARVEST

ONCE UPON A TIME
WHEN THE HARVEST CAME
THERE HAD BEEN
A SHORTAGE OF RAIN

A DROUGHT ENCOMPASSED
MUCH OF THE LAND
DESOLATION HAD ONCE AGAIN
COME UPON MAN

YET A HARVEST
IT WAS AT THAT
UPON THE PEOPLE
IT DID REFLECT

THE HARVEST
WAS THE REAPING OF
LIFE AS DETERMINED
FROM UP ABOVE

FOREVER

ONCE UPON A TIME
IN WHAT TOOK FOREVER
PASSED A MOMENT
BETWEEN NOW AND NEVER

FOR THAT
WHICH SHALL NEVER BE
WILL BE FOREVER
BECOMING REALITY

BETWEEN NOW AND NEVER
IS ETERNITY
A MOMENT IN TIME
WE WAIT FOREVER TO SEE

THE BEST

ONCE UPON A TIME
THERE WAS A MAN
WHO STRIVED TO DO
THE BEST HE CAN

HE WAS UNLIKE
ANY OTHER
BECAUSE OF HIS ABILITY
TO GO A STEP FARTHER

SOME SAY HE WAS GIFTED
SOME SAY HE WAS BLESSED
THAT'S WHAT PEOPLE SAY ABOUT YOU
WHEN YOU STRIVE TO DO YOUR BEST

A MAN WITHOUT A SOUL

ONCE UPON A TIME
THERE WAS A MAN WITHOUT A SOUL
NEEDLESS TO SAY
HIS HEART WAS COLD

HE LIVED IN A WORLD
ALL HIS OWN
IT WAS NATURAL FOR HIM
TO BE ALONE

THERE WAS NO WARMTH
IN HIS TOUCH
HIS ONLY LOVE
THAT OF LUST

WHEN HE SPOKE
HE OFTEN CURSED
HE DIDN'T CARE
WHOS' FEELINGS GOT HURT

ALWAYS ON
A NEGATIVE VIBE
BECAUSE HE HAD
NO SOUL INSIDE

TO HIS GRAVE
HE WENT EACH DAY
WITHOUT A SOUL
HE COULD NOT BE SAVED

THE GREATEST THING

ONCE UPON A TIME
THE GREATEST THING HAPPENED
ALL THE PEOPLE IN THE WORLD
FOUND SATISFACTION

SATISFACTION CAME
WITH THE REALIZATION OF
THERE IS NOTHING GREATER
THAN UNIVERSAL LOVE

A PLACE OF NO REALITY

ONCE UPON A TIME
THERE CAME TO BE
A PLACE
OF NO REALITY

THE APPEARANCES OF LIFE
WERE AN ILLUSION
THE WORLD FILLED
WITH CONFUSION

THE PEOPLE OF THE WORLD
WERE ALL DECEIVED
FOR THIS WAS THE WORLD
IN WHICH THEY BELIEVED

IT WAS A WORLD
OF MATERIALISTIC THINGS
AS THE WAY OF LIFE
FOR HUMAN BEINGS

A LONG TIME AGO

ONCE UPON A TIME
I KNOW NOT WHEN
OR HOW THIS POEM
SHOULD ACTUALLY BEGIN

SO LETS GO BACK
WAY BACK IN TIME
AND SEE WHAT
WE CAN FIND

THERE IT IS
JUST AS I THOUGHT
A TIME LOST
A TIME FORGOT

A TIME BEFORE EARTH
AS WE KNEW EARTH TO BE
A TIME OF WHICH
WE HAVE NO MEMORY

Made in the USA
Middletown, DE
28 April 2022

64885609R00091